Kenneth Ulyatt

THE TIME OF THE INDIAN

*'We preferred our own way of
living . . . all we wanted was peace
and to be left alone.'*
– Chief Crazy Horse of the
Oglala Sioux, 1877.

PUFFIN BOOKS
Explorer 15

Acknowledgements

The publishers and author would like to thank the following for their kind permission to reproduce the photographs, paintings and drawings appearing in this book :

Amon Carter Museum, Fort Worth, Texas : pp. 17, 18 and 23 ; British Columbia Provincial Museum : p. 16 ; the Trustees of the British Museum : pp. 8 and 9 ; Field Museum of Natural History, Chicago, sculptress Malvina Hoffman : p. 34 ; Thomas Gilcrease Institute of American History and Art, Tulsa, Oklahoma : pp. 10, 11, 29, 30, 33, 36, 44 and 45 ; Los Angeles County Museum of Natural History, History Division : p. 37 ; the Mansell Collection : pp. 28 and 39 ; Montana Historical Society, Helena : p. 7 ; Museum of the American Indian, Heye Foundation : p. 46 ; Ruth Koerner Oliver : cover, pp. 1, 20, 32 and 48 ; Rare Book Division, The New York Public Library, Astor, Lennox and Tilden Foundation : pp. 24 and 25 ; Royal Ontario Museum, Toronto : pp. 3, 5 and 36 ; Smithsonian Institution, National Anthropological Archives, Bureau of American Ethnology Collection : pp. 36 and 47 ; U.S. Department of the Interior, Washington : p. 6 ; The Walters Art Gallery : pp. 12 and 13 ; Whitney Gallery of Western Art, Cody, Wyoming : pp. 40 and 41 ; Woolaroc Museum, Bartlesville, Oklahoma : p. 21. We would also like to thank Mr E. G. Morton for drawing the maps, and Michael Charlton for the black and white pen sketches.

Quote on pages 1 and 48 from INDIAN ORATORY, compiled by W. C. Vanderwerth, © 1971, University of Oklahoma Press.

Puffin Books: Penguin Books Ltd,
Harmondsworth, Middlesex, England
Penguin Books Inc., 7110 Ambassador Road,
Baltimore, Maryland 21207, U.S.A.
Penguin Books Australia Ltd, Ringwood,
Victoria, Australia
Penguin Books Canada Ltd,
41 Steelcase Road West, Markham, Ontario, Canada
Penguin Books (N.Z.) Ltd,
182–190 Wairau Road, Auckland 10, New Zealand

First published 1975

Text copyright © Kenneth Ulyatt, 1975
Illustrations copyright © Penguin Books Ltd, 1975

Made and printed in Great Britain by
Westerham Press Ltd, Westerham, Kent
Set in Monophoto Imprint

The primitive Indian was a hunter, and it was the search for food which led him out of Asia, across the 'land bridge' into the empty continent of North America tens of thousands of years ago. This picture, painted by George Catlin in the 1830s, shows an Indian on snowshoes hunting moose in the far north of Canada.

They knew the mammoth was dying. The trail through the tangle of dwarf trees lurched from side to side and there was blood on the trampled grass. Already, a man had been sent back to the camp in the west to fetch the women and children; there would be food for everyone by nightfall.

For a long time the great beast stood swaying beside a small pond in a dip in the rolling plain. A breeze stirred the coarse, reddish hair on its flanks and, as the hunters moved to get down-wind, the massive head sank lower until the curling, ten-foot tusks touched the ground.

A dozen spears hung in its neck, their stone points deeply embedded for they had been hurled hard, with considerable courage, at close range. Suddenly, the mammoth's knees buckled, the huge bulk pitched sideways and the shouting, jubilant hunters rushed in.

The entire tribe camped that night beside the body, which rose like a hairy hill out of the tall grass. In the light of the leaping fires, the flames glistening on their bare and bloody

3

limbs, they hacked the flesh from the body, eating until they could barely move. For days they worked on the carcass, stripping it of meat and cracking the bones for the marrow. When they left, carrying as much food as they could, together with portions of the rough hide to make clothing and shelters, they went east.

The trails all led east! There were the marks of the shaggy mammoth, and of the bison which stood seven feet (2 metres) tall and had a spread of horns as wide. There were many kinds of musk ox, elk and moose. The hunters recognized each spoor and urged their followers on.

That was more than 20,000 years ago when the glaciers of the Ice Age, spreading far down into each continent, had sucked up enough water to cause the level of the seas to fall and make a 'land bridge' between Asia and America. Today, that plain has sunk and the two continents are separated by fifty-six miles (80.46 kilometres) of cold, grey, fog-shrouded water called the Bering Straits.

Today, 56 miles of wind-swept, ice-choked water separates Asia and America. This map shows how the two continents were joined when the level of the sea fell between 200 and 300 feet (61–91m) during the Ice Age.

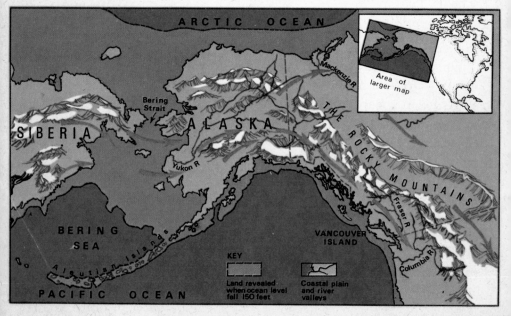

The first Indians, those descendants of the Siberian hunters who had followed the game across the Bering Straits, pushed on in little bands down the river valleys of Alaska and Canada, to the warmer, lusher country where the hunting and living were easier. Paul Kane, the Toronto artist who roved and painted the Canadian west, recorded these Indians fishing on the Columbia River in 1847.

It was warmer there then, and for thousands of years the animals of the Old World wandered across the lush plain of the 'bridge' into the empty Americas. Nobody knows exactly when the first Siberian hunters followed. But in Alaska today, where they are searching for oil, traces of ancient stone fireplaces have been uncovered, and many spear points have been found, like those left embedded in the bones of the mammoth. All this tells of the trails of long ago and proves that this was the route by which the Paleo-Indians – the hunters of more than 10,000 years ago – first came to America.

The beasts that led man to the new continent were grass eaters; big animals that provided a lot of meat at one killing. They moved in large herds, leaving clearly marked trails behind them; trails that led through sheltered valleys where the grazing was good and where there was water in plenty. When they felt the need to cross mountains, they searched for

5

The early settlers in the southwest arrived perhaps 20,000 years ago. They found a contrasting land of forested mountains, colourful deserts and plateaux slashed with twisting rivers. They were a peaceful, hunting people who gradually learned how to irrigate the land and how to grow crops. They built houses of wood and stone, grouped in tight little communities called pueblos (a Spanish word meaning 'town' and pronounced pweb-lo). Sometimes the pueblos were built on flat-topped mountains called mesas, or tucked under the cliffs of a deep canyon, like this famous dwelling at Mesa Verde in Colorado.

the easy passes. And it was by following these game trails that the first hunting Indians found themselves penetrating the very heart of America.

Along the valleys of the Yukon, the Mackenzie and the Peace rivers, and down the Fraser river, the migration went on over thousands of years; not in one great flood, but in small tribal trickles. Driven by the constant search for food and the coming-and-going of the ice-caps, the hunters moved ever southwards to warmer regions where life promised to be easier and the game more plentiful.

One route that the Paleo-Indians followed went down the western side of the great mountain chain, now called the Rockies. It crossed the Columbia River, and moved on to the Great Basin and the southwest. Another route went down the other side of the mountains and discovered the Great Plains, dividing yet again to spread along the mighty rivers into the woodlands of the east.

About 9,000 years ago the seas rose to cover the old 'land

bridge'. By that time, the Ice Age mammoths had gone and so had the big-horned bison, an animal like the two-humped camel, and several others. But man had flourished in the new land. There were Eskimos hunting moose and caribou in the far north; Indians living off the buffalo on the plains; basket-makers and builders in the southwest, and farmers along the eastern coast. Down to Cape Horn, the very land's end of the continent, man was in residence. The time of the Indian had come.

With the melting of the ice and the flooding of the land bridge, great changes had occurred in the New World. Perhaps the biggest change of all happened to the climate. The wet, cloudy skies of the Ice Age had kept the lakes full, the grasses tall and the trees plentiful. Now, high temperatures and scorching sun not only caused many of the rivers and lakes to shrink, but shrivelled up the rich grassland, too.

One route south into the new continent brought the early hunters along the eastern slopes of the Rockies on to the Great Plains. Wandering farmers and hunters, they lived there for untold centuries, following the great herds of buffalo which provided them with food, clothing and shelter. To catch the buffalo they stalked them on foot disguised in animal skins, or stampeded them over a cliff by firing the prairie grass. At this 'buffalo jump' Indians, perched on rocks, wave and shout to drive the animals over the edge. Women and children wait below to sort out the vast pile of dead buffalo.

As their food vanished, the great grass-eating mammoths died off. And as these beasts were the main source of food for the Paleo-Indian hunters they were forced to find a new way to live.

It did not happen right away, and for thousands of years the hunters scratched a meagre living as the game vanished. But by about 8,000 years ago the Indians had established new

By the time the European explorers reached America, the Indians had spread across the entire continent. The largest and most important groupings were those of the northeastern and southeastern woodlands. Three big 'language families' – the Algonquin, the Iroquois and the Muskhogean – occupied a vast territory which stretched from Canada to the Gulf of Mexico, from the Atlantic seaboard to the Mississippi River. John White, who in 1587 went out as Governor of a colony established by Sir Walter Raleigh on Roanoke Island off the coast of North Carolina, described the Indians he met as delightful savages . . . 'gentle, loving and faithful, lacking all guile and trickery . . . as if they lived in a golden age'. Governor White was also an accomplished artist, and his water-colour paintings record the daily life of the Indians of the sixteenth century in painstaking detail. Here, he has shown an Indian chief, his wife and daughter. On the right, is the town of Secoton, with its roads, thatched houses, gardens and cornfields.

ways of life in three distinct parts of the continent . . . ways of life which changed very little until the white man came.

In the southwest were the desert Indians, living at first off wild seeds and roots, lizards, and grass-hoppers. Soon, however, they invented the earth saucepan – a hole in the ground lined with skin or bark. They filled this with water and then dropped in hot stones until the water boiled. Food, which

9

The coming of the white man changed the Indian's way of life, especially with what was called the 'horse culture'. Just as we have quickly become a 'car' people, so the foot Indians suddenly became mobile as horses spread northwards from the Spanish ranches of Mexico. Fortunately there were artists anxious to record these new sights. George Catlin, born in Pennsylvania in 1796, spent eight years in the wilderness. He made this lively sketch of himself, painting a chief of the Mandans, called Ma-to-toh-pa and, right, recorded a Comanche brave 'Catching Wild Horses'.

Alfred Jacob Miller, another painter of the plains, shows very dramatically how the horse helped the Indians to surround and pound the buffalo herds (pages 12 and 13), in contrast to the old buffalo jump.

could be preserved when cooked in this new way, was easily digested by the very young and the very old. The living conditions of the desert dwellers improved. By the time the Spaniards came, in 1540, cotton was growing in the fields, weaving was practised, grain was regularly ground and stored, and many Indians lived in towns of well-built stone houses, four or five stories high.

In the eastern woodlands, the hunters had become farmers. At first, they gathered the food that a generous forest provided freely. But then they discovered that they could use seeds to grow crops both in greater quantity *and* where they wanted them. They made gardens, experimented with irrigation, settled into villages surrounded by farmland. When the European explorers began to move inland from their coastal colonies, they were amazed to find that the woodland Indians grew more plants than the Old World; and that, although

Indian farming methods were different, they were in many ways better than their own! Maize was the main crop, the explorers discovered. But they also found 130 other plants used as food, over 200 for medicines, 25 for dyes, 18 for beverages and flavourings, and 27 for smoking.

Separating the cultures of the southwestern desert and the eastern woodlands were the Great Plains, bare and empty save for the vast herds of buffalo, drifting like clouds over the rolling land. This had been the country of the big-game hunters before the ice sheets melted. Around its edges a small number of tribes still clung to the old way of life.

Wide, muddy rivers stretched like fingers from the woodlands out on to the prairie. Along the banks lived the plains people, growing a little maize and beans but venturing out into the wilderness to hunt the buffalo. Because they were on foot and the distances were so vast, it was a dangerous and wearisome business. But they needed the meat to add to their limited diet — and they needed just about everything else the buffalo could provide, for clothes, shelter and weapons.

They were a poor people, little different from the Ice-Age hunters. Yet today, the whole world knows the Plains Indian. Proud, picturesque, painted — with bow and arrow poised, and

feathered bonnet streaming in the wind – they stand for the whole Indian nation.

How and why did this change take place?

There were no horses in America when the first Indians arrived, so when they hunted, it was on foot; when they travelled, it was slowly; and when they carried anything, it was limited to the load they could hump on their backs. To this foot-slogging people, the Great Plains must have looked like an ocean to men who had no ships – forbidding, unexplored and dangerous.

In 1540, the Spaniards brought horses to the New World. They conquered all Mexico and then gradually extended the kingdom of New Spain northwards. At their *ranchos* and missions in Texas and New Mexico they bred horses; but they would not sell them to the Indians. In 1680, however, the Pueblo Indians rose against their conquerors, drove out the Spanish soldiers and priests, and captured the horse herds.

Being a settled people, these desert Indians did not have much use for the horse. They called it an 'elk dog' and preferred to eat it rather than learn to ride it. In the years that followed more horses were stolen, bartered, and passed from tribe to tribe. Many went wild and roamed out on to the plains; the *mestenos* or 'wild ones', the Spaniards called them. Our word is mustang!

But to the Plains Indians – those wandering people scratching a living, half at farming, half at running after the buffalo – the horse meant power and freedom.

Up through Apache and Comanche country it spread like wildfire. Through the mountains to the Shoshoni and then north to the land of the Blackfeet galloped the new way of life. Horse trading became an Indian profession; wealth was calculated by the number of horses a man possessed. Instead of a trudging foot-people confined to the fringe of the prairies, the Plains Indians quickly became the finest riders in the world.

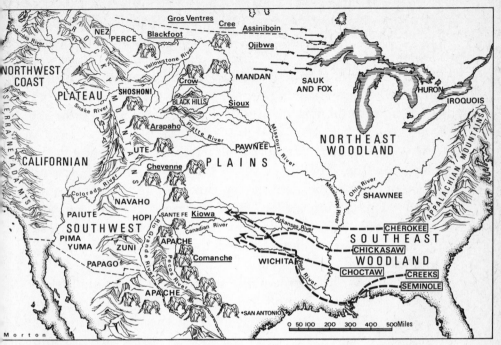

The main groupings of the old Indian cultures; in each area housing, clothing, food and tribal customs were similar. Some of the important tribes are shown in capital letters, while the roving warriors who dominated the plains in the nineteenth century are in small letters and underlined. The horse and gun symbols show the routes by which they spread among the Indians and the arrows trace the removal of the eastern tribes on to the prairie.

In a sudden blaze of mobility they poured out on to the plains. Farming was forgotten. On horseback they could travel vast distances. With these wonderful beasts they could carry all their belongings easily, and kill more buffalo than they had ever dreamed possible. Comanche, Kiowa, Cheyenne, Arapahoe, Sioux, Nez Perce, Blackfoot . . . soon the plains were divided among these mobile, warrior tribes.

The most daring of them all were, perhaps, the Comanches, who rapidly became lords of all the southern plains. George Catlin, who painted the pictures on pages 10 and 11, wrote in a book about his adventures: 'The Comanches [are] the most

15

extraordinary horsemen that I have seen yet in all my travels, and I doubt very much whether any people in the world can surpass them. A Comanche on his feet is out of his element . . . awkward as a monkey on the ground . . . but the moment he lays his hands upon his horse his *face* even becomes handsome, and he gracefully flies away like a different being.'

So the familiar, feathered warrior, sweeping along the prairie skyline, became a symbolic figure. And he was to dominate the scene completely throughout the nineteenth century. But during the long period of pre-history there were many other cultures spread over this vast northern continent, for well over 9 million Indians lived between the Arctic Ocean and the Rio Grande.

As the people who had crossed the Bering Straits from Asia moved slowly down into America, small streams trickled away from the great southward tide of migration. In the far north, the Eskimos settled to a life amidst the ice and snow. Further down the west coast, where fiords slashed the cliffs and islands dotted the misty sounds, a vigorous people grew rich on fish and furs. They decorated their war canoes with fierce animal designs and erected fantastically-carved totem poles in front of their wooden houses. They were the northwest coastal tribes, the Tsimshian, the Nootka, the Salish, the Chinook.

Separated by the mountains and deserts from these busy people in the north and the pueblo builders in the southwest, the Californian Indians lived easily in a warm climate which did not spur them on to any great effort to reach a higher stage of civilization. And in the Great Basin formed by the Rocky Mountains and the Sierra Nevada range

After travelling more than 3,000 miles (4,830km) through largely unexplored country, the Lewis and Clark Expedition reached the Lower Columbia River in November 1805. Charles Russell's painting recaptures the scene and shows the expedition's Indian guide, a young girl of 17, 'talking' in sign language to the Chinook Indians in their decorated canoe. On the opposite page is one of the totem poles of the northwest coast.

were the people who spoke the Shoshonean tongue. A few, living near the Grand Teton Mountains, were rich and showy in their dress. The rest were poor and primitive; grubbing out a miserable existence on roots and wild seeds, small insects and reptiles.

Mark Twain, travelling by stage coach into the Nevada Desert in 1861, described the Gosiutes as 'the wretchedest type of mankind I have ever seen . . . [a people] who produce nothing . . . whose only shelter is a rag cast on a bush to keep off a portion of the snow.'

Across the length and breadth of this land we now call America, there lived then a large population of Indians, speaking many languages, divided into many nations and sub-divided into hundreds of tribes.

No great mechanical inventions came from them. No vast engineering schemes, like railways, motorways, or dams, scarred their land or altered the course of their rivers. Yet the woodland Indians were very clever farmers and many inventions, such as the tobacco pipe, the hollow rubber ball, the toboggan, and a form of central heating for their council halls, originated with the Indians. The difficult surgical operation of trepanning – cutting a circular piece of bone out of the skull to reach the brain – was first performed in the New World. And the Iroquois, in the seventeenth century, had already reached a remarkable understanding of the meaning of dreams, a science that the western world was not to discover until modern times and call 'psychoanalysis'.

It was a woman's job to bring home the buffalo meat or move camp. For this, she made a travois, *an A-shaped frame of long poles lashed together with buffalo rawhide. The loose ends supported the load dragged behind the pony. Sometimes dogs dragged small travois, too. Painting by Charles M. Russell.*

But above all, the Indian had learned to live in harmony with nature. Only the surplus food was cropped each season; only enough animals killed to fill his immediate needs. It was a striking achievement, this balance with nature, and in his dances, songs and daily rituals he expressed his relationship to the sun, the wind, the water and the sky. In particular, he sought the help of the animals, great and small. By adopting their names, wearing their skins, decorating his tepee and weapons with their symbol, he hoped to gain for himself something of their special skills.

In short, the Indian used everything that nature provided to the full but never took more than he needed. Unknowingly, instinctively, he was a great conservationist.

Until the white man came.

The Indians were a puzzle to the early explorers of the New World. Pushing into the woodlands, claiming the land for their king's glory and their own profit, the Europeans saw the people they encountered as a simple race, lacking the cleverness and 'push' that had made the trading countries of the Old World so rich and powerful.

Yet there were thoughtful men, particularly among the French, who looked at the woodland tribes and saw a sort of golden age; a contented, happy way of life that Europe, with its wars and oppression, famines and plagues, had somehow lost track of. They called the Indian 'the noble savage', and shipped some willing chiefs back to the court at Versailles.

An Indian craze swept Europe as these strange, dignified men, in full feathered regalia and warpaint, posed for the white artists. The Indian Princess, Pocahontas, was taken to England in about 1616 and baptized as Lady Rebecca. She was a sensation. Indians, as we would say today, were 'in', the trendy thing to know about.

But to the colonists living along the eastern coast of America they remained an inferior and sometimes dangerous

here were attempts to teach them Christianity, it is
ut from the very beginning the Indians were in the
nd it was not very long before the white men began to
pus.. .iem west.

The Spaniards had already conquered Mexico in a crazy
quest for gold. Moving north, they subdued the Californian
Indians and then began to settle the southwest, building
missions and laying out great *ranchos*. In the east, the British
and French, who had been busy fighting each other across the
length and breadth of Europe, now began to fight each other
for possession of the New World. And between the red-
coated armies, whose cannon brought a strange, new thunder
to echo among the peaceful hills, the Indians were caught in a
deadly trap.

*In the eastern woodlands, the settlers, who wanted to farm and hold the land for their
own, came face to face with the Indians, who loved to hunt and roam at will.
W. H. D. Koerner's painting, 'Sauk's Demand', dramatically illustrates the conflict
between members of that tribe and the pioneers. Note the butter churn beside the door.*

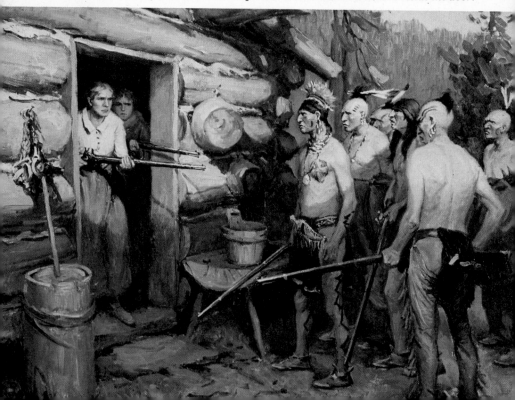

The first white men to live among the Indians were the fur trappers. Once a year they held a rendezvous on the slopes of the Rockies to receive supplies from the east and to trade in their pelts. Alfred Jacob Miller, a young American artist, accompanied one such supply expedition to the Green River in 1837 and recorded this exciting scene.

Driven out by the colonists (who found it easier to take Indian fields and villages rather than clear new land), their hunting grounds disturbed by the fur trappers, the Indian couldn't begin to understand the white man's greed. The very idea of owning vast areas of land was strange to him, and the desire to take so much from nature – trapping the beaver for its pelt until the animal almost died out, taking crop after crop from the fields and moving on to fresh land, felling acres of the forest for wood – all this seemed to go against everything that the Indian held sacred.

And, in the war of 1763, when both French and British tricked and bribed the tribes into taking sides, the treachery, humiliation and cruelty reached new heights.

It is sad to record that when a chief named Pontiac, fighting for the French, fell upon the English forts at Detroit, it was a British commander who ordered the distribution among the Indians of handkerchiefs and blankets from the smallpox hospital at Fort Pitt in the hope of infecting them with the disease.

At last, the colonists became tired of fighting Europe's wars and rebelled to form an independent United States. Thirteen colonies, from Georgia in the south to Massachusetts in the north, joined together to make one country. And as their western border they took the great Mississippi river. It signalled the end for the woodland tribes when even the great American statesman and philosopher Benjamin Franklin joined in the game 'to extirpate these savages in order to make room for the cultivators of the earth'.

With the British defeated, and a vast new land, Louisiana, bought from the French in the west, the young United States had no further need for their Indian allies. With great speed they set about exploring their huge country – for much of it was unknown – and encouraging settlement further and further into the west.

The Indians, however, had no intention of tamely giving up the lands which had been theirs for centuries. The Pueblos had already risen against the Spaniards in 1680; and in 1762, Pontiac had united the Ottawas, Chippewas, Hurons, Potawatomis and other tribes around the Great Lakes to fight the British.

Now, as the Americans began to move into the Ohio valley and bargain with the individual tribes for their lands, a Shawnee chief named Tecumseh was quick to see the danger that threatened. 'Sell a country!' he cried. 'Why not sell the air, the clouds, the sea . . . did not the Great Spirit make them for the use of all his children?'

Visiting every tribe from the headwaters of the Missouri to

*Horses and guns! The Indians
received little else from their c[...]
with white civilization. They could no[...]
understand the white man's idea of
wealth; they suffered terribly from his
diseases; they were the constant victims
of his treachery. As the frontier moved
even further westwards, and ranches and
farms sprang up on the great plains
themselves, the tribes prepared to defend
their last hunting grounds. It was to be a
series of savage wars which they could
not possibly win. But they were going to
fight! And more horses and more guns
were the first things they needed.*

*This detail is taken from a painting by
Charles Russell and shows Navajo
Indians stealing horses from the
Mexican settlements.*

the Rockies, and travelling as far south as Florida, he tried to rouse the Indians and encouraged them to arm themselves against the white invader. But before they were really ready, his younger brother launched an attack at Tippecanoe on the Wabash River and was quickly defeated. Two years later, Tecumseh was killed while fighting for the British in Ontario. His dream of a united Indian nation remained just a dream.

Gradually, the Indians retreated before the tide of westward expansion. The Iroquois fled to Canada. The Seminoles vanished into the swamps of Florida and held the United States Army at bay for seven years. The Sauks and Foxes fought a futile war led by Black Hawk, who was tricked into giving away his Illinois village by being made to 'touch the quill' to a document he did not understand.

But not all the tribes chose the warpath.

In the mountains, where Georgia, Tennessee and North Carolina meet, the Cherokees decided to follow the white man's ways. They built roads, churches and schools, and

The golden age of the Plains Indians
arrived with the horse. No longer did they
have to grow maize and beans and
pumpkins along the edges of the rivers. No
longer did they chase the buffalo on foot – a
slow and laborious game. Now, the whole
tribe followed the hunt and, with their
entire existence dependent on the herds,
they invented dances and ceremonies which
they believed would give them power over
the great beasts. In 1835, a German prince,
Maximilian, travelled up the Missouri
with a young Swiss artist, Carl Bodmer.
The scenes of Indian life which Bodmer
painted are among the finest ever made.
Here is the buffalo dance of the Mandans,
in which some of the dancers are wearing
huge masks made out of an entire buffalo's
head. They have painted their bodies and
tied on tails behind, and their dance
imitates the movements of the buffalo. This
'buffalo calling' went on for days, in the
hope of luring the herds closer to the village.

The many gods of the Indians dwelt in
natural things like mountains, rivers,
rainbows – and in the hundreds of
animals of the west. Each tribe had secret
societies named after these spirits. Prince
Maximilian listed many of them : the Kit
Foxes, Black Mouths, Bulls, Ravens,
Little Dogs . . . and Carl Bodmer painted
this striking picture of a Minnitaree
warrior in the costume of the Dog Dance.

worked out a style of government based on that of the brand-
new United States. A chief named Sequoya invented a
Cherokee alphabet, and soon this remarkable Indian nation
had its own printing press and newspaper. By 1826 there were
Cherokee farms, saw mills, and blacksmith shops; the women
made their European-type dresses from their own cotton, and
even the men wore flowing tunic-shirts and turbans. They

Just as a soldier gets a medal, so Indians were awarded eagle feathers for brave deeds, or 'coups'. A single feather, tufted with horsehair, marked the first coup; red bars were added for more coups. A spot indicated an enemy killed; a notch meant a scalp taken or a throat cut. A feather split down the middle showed that the brave had received many wounds.

hoped that they could live alongside the colonists in peace and enjoy the benefits of white civilization.

There were five such 'civilized' tribes: the Choctaw, Creek, Chickasaw, Seminole and Cherokee. But their dreams were doomed.

Already, long ago, an Indian agent, appointed by the American Secretary for War, had travelled through highland Georgia. He described this mild and pleasant land, but then reported that its beauties and natural resources 'were rendered unpleasant by being in the possession of the jealous natives' and that the land 'must, in the process of time, become part of the United States'.

By 1830, that time had come. In that year, President Andrew Jackson, who had grown up on the frontier and who had little time for the rights of Indians, signed the Removal Act.

War party leader.   *Killed enemy in hand-to-hand fight.*   *Helped to defend a camp.*   *Coup marks.*   *Took part in horse raids.*

Quite simply, this stated that all Indians living east of the Mississippi must leave their homes and move westwards out on to the prairie.

The Seminoles fought. The Chickasaws and Choctaws went resignedly. The 'trail of tears', as it was to be called, had begun. The removal went on for years. The Creeks, having signed a treaty which said that they could go or stay, just as they wished, were then driven from their lands with their chiefs in chains.

Finally, even the Cherokees gave in. In the winter of 1835 they moved west. A few tried to cling to their farms, schools and libraries but the soldiers fell on them, looting and burning.

No one knows the toll exacted by the Trail of Tears – how many died from disease, exposure and starvation. But by the end of 1836 nearly 100,000 Indians had been resettled on the plains in a brutal operation the like of which the civilized world was not to see again until the Nazis swept across Europe.

So the eastern woodlands were cleared of their original owners. The frontier halted on the Mississippi. The stage was set for the final drama.

It had taken 200 years to drive the Indians from the

The Indians painted themselves for many reasons. They had their own personal designs (like Crazy Horse's hailstone war paint) when they went to fight. They painted themselves for protection against frost and snow and insect bites ; even to treat skin diseases ! This Sioux warrior, returning from a raid, has blackened his face to show that the fires of his revenge are burned out. A wound is circled with the healing rays of the sun ; on his arms are 'coup' marks. His pony would be painted too, and some of the symbols are shown opposite.

Atlantic coast to the prairies beyond the Mississippi. For a short time, it seemed as if the white man would be satisfied with what he had taken; the westward-rolling frontier halted along the length of the great river, and the Indians who had survived the removal gradually settled down to a new life on the plains.

Thirteen tribes ruled the grasslands in the early nineteenth

They were great sportsmen – and gamblers – these warriors of the plains, organizing fiercely competitive horse races, archery contests and a game called 'lacrosse'. This was the name given by the French fur traders to the webbed sticks with which the players caught a deerskin ball and tried to hurl it through high goalposts. Hundreds of Indians played at a time and everybody would bet on the result of the game.

In 1834, George Catlin drew this picture of Choctaw Indians playing the traditional game which they had brought to the plains from their original home in the east.

On 28 May 1830, President Jackson signed the Indian Removal Act. Under its terms all tribes east of the Mississippi had to give up the land which had been theirs for centuries and move west. Escorted by soldiers, their chiefs in chains, it was a 'trail of tears'. Robert Lindneux painted this sad picture.

century. They ranged from the Cheyenne and the Sioux in the north – tribes which had been driven there from the wooded country near the Great Lakes – to the Apache and Comanche in the south – tribes which had moved out of Mexico in an effort to get away from the Spaniards.

For a brief time these mounted warriors roamed the plains at will, fighting amongst themselves for territory or even for sport. You have heard many of their names in stories and in films; you can trace where they lived on the map on page 15.

The Indian's whole way of life depended on the vast herds of buffalo, which gave him nearly everything he needed. Food, shelter, social customs, wealth . . . all came from this shaggy beast.

The tough, thick hide of the old bulls he used for his shields and for the soles of his moccassins. With the pliable, thinner cowhide he covered his tepee. He made ceremonial rattles and masks from hoofs and horns, and bowstrings and arrowheads from sinews and bones. From the paunch, his wife made a cooking pot or a bucket; from the tail, a fly swish. And she used the rough side of the tongue as a hairbrush. Calfskin balls were sewn together to amuse the warrior's children, and he used rawhide for the bridle, saddle and rigging of his horse. He used it too, to make snowshoes when the winter came, and he fashioned sledge runners from the long buffalo ribs. Other bones made knives, ladles, spoons, sewing awls, and dice for gambling. Even the buffalo dung was dried and used as fuel on the treeless plain!

From one year's end to another, the hunters followed the

River steamboats, railway engines, the telegraph . . . these were the things which made the white conquest of the west so swift, so inevitable. William Cary, a New York artist, made several trips beyond the frontier in 1860 when he painted this picture of a group of amazed Indians watching 'The Fire Canoe' on the Missouri River.

buffalo. When the hunting was good, then life was good. And so numerous were the herds, so vast in number, that the hunt rarely failed. For about 100 years, the Plains Indian lived richly and freely, and his pictures, legends, and ceremonies nearly all deal with the twin sources of his wealth and freedom – the buffalo and the horse.

Life on the plains was not that easy. The Indians lived close to nature. They travelled long distances under the hot summer sun, and suffered in the winter, when snowy winds sent the temperature plunging way down below freezing point.

But the children worked and played in the open air all the time, and soon took part in the life of the tribe. By the age of five or six, the boys would be good riders, helping with the horse herds and preparing for the hunt. Like boys anywhere, their games copied the activities of the adults; and by imitation hunts, make-believe raids, and shooting with small bows and arrows, they soon became pretty good at the skills they would need when they were called into the service of the tribe. The girls played with toy dolls and made cradles and miniature tepees, learning to sew and cook, and preparing themselves for courtship and marriage.

By the time a boy was twelve, he would be riding with his father on real hunts, and in his early teens, he might go on a war party. His job would be to help with the chores around the camp and to tend the horses, but he would also watch the warriors in action and, if things did not go well, might end up fighting for his life.

War, when he grew old enough to take part in it, became his whole life. Not so much a means of conquering territory or of vanquishing other tribes, war was a way of obtaining what you wanted – whether it was horses, guns or women. Most important of all, war enabled the young warrior to gain prestige, for who would want to marry him if he had not been to war, or listen to him if he could not recount his deeds in battle?

Scalps were taken to show that a warrior had been successful in killing an enemy, but more important than killing was the scoring of a *coup* – that is, the touching or striking of an enemy with the hand or a special stick, during the fight.

The whole process of war, like the hunt, was highly organized within the tribe, and when he was old enough, a warrior would be invited to join one of the soldier societies. Only the Plains Indians had such societies, and each one had its own particular name. There were the Foolish Dogs and Crazy Dogs of the Mandan and Hidatsa, the Crazy Lodges of the Arapaho, the Red Shields and Fox Soldiers of the Cheyenne, and the Koitsenko – or the Ten Bravest – of the Kiowa. The chiefs made them responsible for law and order in the camp and on the hunt, but the main reason for the creation of the soldier societies was war!

They all had ceremonial dances, songs and costume; the

Whisky and white soldiers! In the early 1800s the golden age of the Plains Indian began to pale before the white invasion. Wagon trains brought settlers to the prairie; traders used whisky to 'soften up' their customers; the buffalo herds shrank under the onslaught of the hide hunters ... and in the wake of the settlers came the soldiers, to build forts and protect the new roads. W. H. D. Koerner painted this picture of a trader's 'palaver'.

Another great Western artist, O. C. Seltzer, made this lively little sketch of the construction of the first fort on the Yellowstone (see facing page).

most important item of dress being a sash, which was worn across the shoulder with the end wound up and tucked under one arm. A 'dog soldier' was pledged to lead the charges and fight in the front rank of every battle. It was his duty, when things were going badly, to encourage those around him by unrolling his sash and pinning it to the ground with a ceremonial arrow. This was a sign that he would not move from that spot until he was killed or unpinned by another member of the society.

There were many customs to be observed by the 'dog soldiers' but 'no flight' or 'no retreat' was the boast of each warrior. He was proud of his appearance and of his standing in the camp, and this is reflected in this description of a Hidatsa warrior whose relatives had been killed in a Sioux attack.

'I am going to die. I will become a Crazy Dog!' He bought red flannel for the sashes . . . he made a rattle out of a buffalo paunch and tied eagle feathers to one end of it . . . he wore a fine war bonnet on his head and tied skunk-skin ornaments to his moccassins. His necklace was of bapa'ce shells . . . in the back he wore a switch and in the front little braids of hair. He rode a fine spotted horse with docked tail; for its trappings he sewed together red and green flannel. When he rode through the camp he began to sing and the old women cheered him. He was killed in battle.*

The price of membership of a warrior society was usually high. In one fight with their enemies, the Crows, a Sioux soldier society lost eighteen of its twenty-two members, the remaining four being dragged away, wounded.

This was the pattern of Indian life when a sudden explosion set the frontier rolling westwards once more.

There had been expeditions across the new country long before the Removal. In 1804, President Jefferson had sent his Corps of Discovery, led by Captains Meriwether Lewis and

*R. H. Lowie, *Military Societies of the Crow Indians* (1916).

Many tribes, many tongues, brought 'hand talk' into common use. Here are a few signs from this versatile language.

1. True, or straight talk. Push index finger in and out in a straight line from chin.

2. Yes. Hold right index finger up, pull quickly downwards towards body.

3. No. Right hand flat against chest; push away in wide half-circle, fingers pointing outwards, palm turning up.

William Clark, 'to explore the Missouri River & such principal stream of it, as, by its course & communication with the waters of the Pacific Ocean . . . may offer the most direct & practical water communication across this continent for the purposes of commerce'.

Two years later, Lieutenant Zebulon M. Pike left St Louis to explore the southern border of the Louisiana Territory. Traders and trappers were quick to follow. The American and Pacific Fur Company set up a post in Oregon in 1808, and by 1826, William Sublette had hauled a mule cart across the mountains to break the first leg of the Oregon Trail.

By 1830 – the time of the Removal Act – the busy northwest culture had begun to break up under the influence of white settlers, who spread alcohol and disease among the Indians. California had long been settled. And with the Trail of Tears from the east, the great plains became the last refuge of the native peoples of America.

But even these vast, empty spaces were threatened, and the

4. Eat. Palm downwards, curve right hand towards lips; push downwards several times.

5. Good. Place right hand against left breast, palm down. Push away from body, swinging upwards to indicate heart soaring.

6. Bad. Clench fist of right hand, hold against left breast, pull downwards to right, opening hand in sweeping movement.

The proud fighters of the plains posed willingly for the pioneer artists of the west and these magnificent portraits give a glimpse of the colourful native costume which so fascinated the early explorers. Above left : The Cree chief, 'Man Who Gives the War-Whoop', holds a sacred pipe as he poses for Paul Kane in 1848. Below : Young Omahaw, War Eagle, Little Missouri and Pawnees pose for Charles Bird King in 1821. Top right : Kicking Bear, the Sioux chief who fought Custer and took part in the Ghost Dance War, painted by Henry H. Cross, probably about 1890 when he was with Buffalo Bill Cody's wild west show.

The camera, however, was another matter. When William S. Soule took these early photographs at Fort Sill, Oklahoma, in 1869, he had to explain that the glass eye in the little black box only borrowed one's face and then returned it to the owner with a copy on paper. Even then the Indians wondered how often a man could lend his face before he lost it

altogether! Soule managed to take many portraits, working under difficult conditions. You can see where one of the glass negatives has cracked. From left to right: Woman Heart and Satanta (or White Bear), Kiowa chiefs. Below, Tashawah and Esatonyett, Comanches. Note how the white man's hat and medals have replaced the finery of the earlier paintings.

sudden explosion – the railway – signalled the end. It had taken 200 years for the frontier to reach the Mississippi, less than halfway across the continent. With the coming of the river steamboat, the railway, and the telegraph, the remaining distance to the Pacific coast was to be leaped in a few decades.

For the Indian, it meant almost seventy years of continuous war!

It began in the heart of Apache country, where the Mexicans were mining the hills for copper. To clear out the Indians, a bounty of $100 was offered for every Apache scalp. A trader named James Johnson invited chiefs of the tribe to a feast in Santa Rita, but he secretly placed a howitzer behind a screen of branches and blasted the unsuspecting Indians with a charge of bullets, nails and pieces of chain.

From this incident sprang the Apache's great hatred of the 'white eyes', and for over thirty years, led by a succession of famous chiefs – Mangas Coloradas, Victorio, Cochise, Geronimo – they fought the miners and soldiers who were trying to oust them from their country.

Far to the north a similar invasion was taking place in the Minnesota River Valley. In a sudden, savage uprising, the Indians burned farms and slaughtered the farmers and their families. The rising was put down by the Army with a public mass-hanging of thirty-eight Sioux Indians at Fort Snelling.

The Cheyenne, also, were driven from their homes by fire and sabre. At Sand Creek in Colorado, a fanatical cavalry commander, Colonel Chivington, fell upon an Indian wintering village where the chief, Black Kettle, was flying an American flag, at peace with the whites. The cavalrymen killed women and children indiscriminately, in what has since been described officially as 'the foulest and most unjustifiable crime in the annals of America'.

Many other wrongs were perpetrated against the Indians. Sharp Knife, as they called President Andrew Jackson, had

For twenty years the Indians retreated before the white invaders. But when the Army advanced on the last Sioux stronghold, beyond the Powder River, they struck back. Colonel Custer, force-marching the 7th Cavalry day and night, reached the Indian camp first. But on the Little Big Horn River, faced with an overwhelming horde of warriors, his luck ran out.

promised the tribes that all the country west of the Mississippi would be Indian Territory. No white man would be permitted to settle on it; no traders allowed in without a licence. Yet, hardly was the ink dry on this treaty than the whites found reason to invade the land.

Maybe it was the copper of Santa Rica, maybe the gold of California. Maybe it was the very grass itself . . . the reasons always seemed good ones and the whites invented a phrase which covered all the deceptions – *Manifest Destiny.* 'It was our manifest destiny to overspread the continent allotted by Providence for the free development of our yearly multiplying millions', wrote one newspaper in 1845. In stronger language this meant: permission given by God to move west, and to hell with any Indian in the way. The tide of expansion rolled on.

Divided, bewildered, the tribes fought back. The accounts of their battles fill many books. But what happened to the

Frederic Remington drew these pictures of (above) Indian scouts watching the advancing soldiers and (left) a trooper unhorsed during the attack. On the next pages is Edgar S. Paxson's painting of the final moments of the battle. Made after years of research on the scene, it shows the last charge, when Crazy Horse and his Oglala warriors swept down the barren hill side and overran the remnants of Custer's force.

39

Sioux will stand for what happened to all the Indian nations –
wherever they fought their last fight.

The Sioux held all the land north of the Platte River;
something they had achieved by treaty under their resolute
old chief, Red Cloud, at Fort Phil Kearny in 1866.

In 1874, however, a strange expedition set out for the Black
Hills of Dakota in defiance of the Government treaty. It was
led by Colonel Custer, a dashing cavalry commander whose
men had eventually killed old Black Kettle at the Battle of

Washita. The purpose of the expedition was a military reconnaissance; but Custer took with him miners, geologists, and newspapermen. What he seemed to be looking for was gold, and in the *Pah-sap-pa*, as the Indians called their sacred hills, the expedition found it.

Immediately Custer sent his most trusted scout, 'Lonesome' Charley Reynolds, racing south to Fort Laramie with a glowing report that the hills were full of gold 'from the grass roots down'. The news swept the country like wildfire and

from every part gold-hungry men headed for the Black Hills.

Dismayed, the Sioux tried to halt the invasion. There were peace councils at which the Government offered to buy the Hills for a mere $400,000. But the shadow of Tecumseh loomed over the council tents.

'I will kill the first Indian who talks favourably of selling the *Pah-sap-pa*,' cried Crazy Horse, warrior chief of the Oglala Sioux. The meeting broke up in disorder. Some Indians returned to the camp grounds beside the forts along the Platte, but more, many more, headed west for Crazy Horse's camp on the Powder River. And from there, they struck back . . . at the trespassing prospectors, at the stage coaches, at isolated farms and ranches south of the river. By the spring of 1876 the Government had had enough and set out to teach the Sioux a lesson.

From Fort Ellis in Montana came General Gibbon. From Fort Fetterman in the south came General Crook. And from Fort Abraham Lincoln in the east came Generals Terry and Custer . . . nearly 3,000 men, marching in three strong columns, due to rendezvous below the Big Horn Mountains and crush the Indians in between.

Crook stumbled on the Sioux first, on the banks of the Rosebud. But Crazy Horse had good scouts; he knew Crook was coming and laid an ambush. Shaken, after a four-hour

Painted Sioux war ponies. Lightning flashes to give the horse speed; 'coup' marks and the records of horse raids; special warrior society markings which helped keep the members together in battle. These, and the designs shown on pages 26 and 27 are recorded in Thomas E. Mails wonderful book, The Mystic Warriors of the Plains.

battle, Crook retreated, sent couriers back to Fort Fetterman, and made camp.

On the Yellowstone, Terry and Gibbon were in conference. The trail of a war party had been discovered, running up the Rosebud valley. There was no news, of course, from Crook, but the commanders sensed that the Indian army was near by, in one of the little river valleys that ran down from the mountains.

Terry ordered Custer to follow the trail, while he and Gibbon marched on a parallel course up the Big Horn River. Whoever found the Sioux first would halt, send scouts to the other command, and wait until a united attack could be mounted.

But Custer was a glory hunter. He force-marched his men forty miles a day, and from the Wolf Divide, the ridge of hills separating the Rosebud from the Little Big Horn, his scouts saw signs of the Indian camp. Trees and a line of bluffs hid the tepees, but Mitch Bouyer, the half-breed scout who wore two stuffed birds on either side of his skin cap, reported 'plenty Indians – for everybody!'

Custer had no intention of waiting for Terry. He marched down into the valley with pennons flying, and on the bank of the river he divided his command: Captain Benteen and three companies were sent up the valley to block any possible Indian retreat, and Major Reno was ordered to take his three companies across the river and to charge the camp. Custer, with five companies left, promised: 'You will be supported by the whole outfit.' But as soon as Reno took his men into the

The end of the trail was reached in 1890 with the Ghost Dance War. In this strange, religious movement, the Indians were promised the return of the buffalo and long-dead friends and relatives. And a new land would come, rolling the whites back into the eastern sea from which they came. Praying and dancing the Ghost Dance and singing the Ghost Dance songs, the tribes prepared for the new life. Ghost shirts were painted with mystic designs that each warrior believed would turn away the white soldiers' bullets.

more well-equipped troops, backed by artillery, moved into the field against them, resistance melted away.

A tale of surrender, treachery and murder followed. Crazy Horse, American Horse, Sitting Bull, and other great chiefs, all died in tragic circumstances.

For brief moments the red man's star shone. Chief Joseph led the Nez Perce from Oregon nearly to the borders of Canada, fighting off more than 5,000 troops on the way, before he surrendered. Dull Knife and Little Wolf outwitted the armies of four Generals when they took the deported Cheyenne back to their homeland, 1,000 miles away.

But the end was near. As the whites divided up the land only dreams were left.

In the winter of 1889 these dreams took shape through the visions of a Paiute sheep herder in Nevada. He claimed that God had told him that the old way of life would return, and the white men be swept into the sea, if only the Indians would give up their warlike ways and dance for peace.

The idea spread like a fever through the shattered Indian nations – until Christmas, 1890. On 29 December, Big Foot and his band of Sioux, who had been dancing the Ghost Dance, were called upon to surrender at Wounded Knee. Surrounding them were units of the 7th Cavalry, with four Hotchkiss guns trained upon the resentful Indians.

As two soldiers struggled to disarm an Indian called Black Coyote, his rifle went off. Custer's old regiment eagerly opened fire, and when the smoke had cleared and the screaming ceased nearly 200 Indians – men, women and babies – lay huddled in the snow.

So the trail ended in bloodshed and bitterness. There were no more treaties, for the Indians had lost everything. There were no more battles, for the will to fight had gone as well.

By the end of the century the hunters who had come, so long ago, down into this great continent, making it their own, respecting the life around them, and content with its natural beauties as they found them, had almost vanished. From 10,000,000 people their numbers had shrunk to 250,000, and these survivors were huddled upon reservations occupying no more than 200,000 square miles. The whites, over 40,000,000 strong, held over three million square miles.

The time of the Indian was over.

At Wounded Knee, South Dakota, just after the Christmas of 1890, the Sioux again confronted the 7th Cavalry. But the Ghost Shirts didn't stop any bullets and when the battle was over many men, women and children were dead. They lay on the snow-covered field for three days until a burial party came. The Ghost Shirts were stripped off as souvenirs and the corpses heaped in a mass grave. Then the white men posed for this picture. Then they shovelled the dirt into the pit and rode away. It was the end of the Sioux nation.

A Reading List

One of the best books I have ever seen on this subject is *The American Heritage Book of Indians*. It tells the whole story in detail, with hundreds of fine pictures. But this recommendation raises a problem; the best books on Indians are usually American. You really will have to search your library shelves or talk to the librarian.

I have written about the Sioux wars in *North Against the Sioux* and *Custer's Gold*. Puffin publish *When the Legends Die* by Hal Borland and also Grey Owl's *Pilgrims of the Wild*. There is *The True Book about North American Indians* by A. B. Campbell; *The First Book of Indian Wars* by R. B. Morris . . . and my library had *Homesteaders and Indians* by Dorothy Levenson, an American book. But perhaps you feel up to trying some grown-up histories. In that case, *Bury My Heart at Wounded Knee* by Dee Brown, *Warriors on Horseback* by Stephen Longstreet and Paul Wellman's *Death on the Prairie* . . . all recent paperbacks.

'*I was born upon the prairie, where the wind blew free, and there was nothing to break the light of the sun. I was born where there were no enclosures and where everything drew a free breath. I want to die there . . . and not within walls.*'

Chief Ten Bears, a Comanche, at the Medicine Lodge Council of 1867.